Romantic Rendezvous

S0-BPT-225

Great Quotations Publishing Company

Compiled by Peggy Schaffer
Cover Art and Design by: Jeff Maniglia

Copyright © 1992 by Great Quotations Publishing

All rights reserved. No part of this book may be
reproduced or transmitted in any form or by any means,
electronic or mechanical, including photocopying, recording
or by any information storage and retrieval system, without
permission in writing from the publisher.

Published in the United States by:
Great Quotations Publishing Co.
Lombard, Illinois 60148

Printed in U.S.A.
ISBN 1-56245-060-3

For Joel

*To love is to admire with the heart;
to admire is to love with the mind.*

Gautier (1811-1872)

*Absence extinguishes small passions
and increases great ones,
as the wind will blow out a candle,
and blow in a fire.*

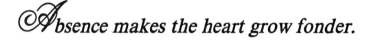 *Absence makes the heart grow fonder.*

*Though we travel the world over
to find the beautiful,
we must carry it with us
or we find it not.*

Ralph Waldo Emerson (1803-1882)

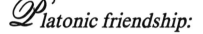*Platonic friendship:*

*The interval between the introduction
and the first kiss.*

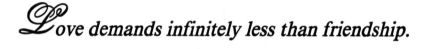

Love demands infinitely less than friendship.

*There is only one quality worse
than hardness of heart
and that is softness of head.*

Theodore Roosevelt

I love thee for a heart that's kind —
Not for the knowledge in thy mind.

W. H. Davies

An advantage of having a hard heart is that it will take a lot to break it.

*The heart has its reasons which
reason does not understand.*

The head never rules the heart,
but just becomes its partner in crime.

Mignon McLaughlin

Some people feel with their heads and think with their hearts.

G. C. Lichtenberg (1742-1799)

The pleasures of the intellect are permanent,
the pleasures of the heart are transitory.

Henry David Thoreau (1817-1862)

*K*indness in words creates confidence.
Kindness in thinking creates profoundness.
Kindness in giving creates love.

Lao-tzu (604?-531 B.C.)

Love doesn't make the world go 'round.
Love is what makes the ride worthwhile.

Franklin P. Jones

He gave her a look you could have poured on a waffle.

*If two people love each other,
there can be no happy end to it.*

Ernest Hemingway

*Many a man has fallen in love with a girl
in a light so dim he would not
have chosen a suit by it.*

Maurice Chevalier

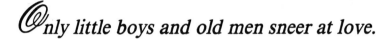 *Only little boys and old men sneer at love.*

Platonic love is love from the neck up.

*People who are sensible about love
are incapable of it.*

Douglas Yates

*Love does not consist in gazing
at each other but in
looking outward together
in the same direction.*

Antoine de Saint Exupery

$\mathscr{C}$*ome live with me and be my love;*
And we will all the pleasures prove.

Christopher Marlowe (1564-1593)

*It's not love's going that hurts my days -
But that it went in little ways.*

Edna St. Vincent Millay

*He was awake a long time before
he knew his heart was broken.*

Ernest St. Vincent Millay

*Marriage is the deep, deep
peace of the double bed
after the hurly burly of
the chaise lounge.*

Mrs. Patrick Campbell

*The honeymoon is over when he phones
that he'll be late for supper —
and she has already left a note
that it's in the refrigerator.*

Bill Lawrence

When singleness is bliss, it's folly to be wives.

Bill Counselman

*Matrimony is a process by which
a grocer acquired an account the florist had.*

Francis Rodman

A man may be a fool and not know it,
but not if he is married.

H. L. Mencken

*One was never married, and that's his hell;
another is, and that's his plague.*

Robert Burton

No matter how happily a
woman may be married,
it always pleases her to discover that
there is a nice man who wishes she were not.

H. L. Mencken

Marriage — a book of which the first chapter is written in poetry and the remaining chapters in prose.

Beverley Nichols

Why does a woman work ten years to change
a man's habits and then complain that
he's not the man she married?

Barbra Streisand

*Love, the quest;
marriage, the conquest;
divorce, the inquest.*

Helen Rowland

When a husband and wife
have got each other,
the devil only knows which has got the other.

Honore de Balzac (1799-1850)

When a girl marries,
she exchanges the attentions of many men
for the inattention of one.

Helen Rowland

A bell is not a bell until you ring it;
A song is not a song until you sing it.
Love in your heart is not put there to stay;
Love is not love until you give it away.

*The great secret of a successful marriage
is to treat all disasters as incidents
and none of the incidents as disasters.*

Harold Nicholson

*Of course there is such a thing as love,
or there wouldn't be so many divorces.*

Ed Howe

*Love is only for the young,
the middle-aged,
and the old.*

I have a wife,
you have a wife, we all have wives,
we've had a taste of paradise,
we know what it means to be married.

Sholem Aleichem

Marriage is a feast where the grace is sometimes better than the dinner.

Charles Caleb Colton

Today, he admits, he gave his sons just
one piece of advice.
"Never confuse I love you with
I want to marry you."

Cleveland Amory

Friendships, like marriages,
are dependent on avoiding the unforgivable.

John D. MacDonald

Often the difference between a successful marriage and a mediocre one consists of leaving about three or four things a day unsaid.

Harlan Miller

Passion is an emotion;
Love is a choice.

*A sound marriage is not
based on complete frankness;
it is based on a sensible reticence.*

Morris L. Ernst

Marriage is a mistake
every man should make.

George Jessel

*The vow of fidelity
is an absurd commitment,
but is the heart of marriage.*

Father Robert Capon

*One should always be in love.
That is the reason one should never marry.*

Oscar Wilde

All marriages are happy.
It's the living together afterward
that causes all the trouble.

Raymond Hull

Niagara Falls is only the second biggest disappointment of the standard honeymoon.

Oscar Wilde

A working girl is one
who quit her job to get married.

E. J. Kiefer

A correspondence course of passion was, for her, the perfect and ideal relationship with a man.

Aldous Huxley

The way to love anything is to realize that it might be lost.

Chesterton

Marriage has many pains but celibacy has no pleasure.

Samuel Johnson

A dress that zips up the back will bring a
husband and wife together.

James H. Boren

Come live with me, and be my love,
And we will some new pleasures prove
Of golden sands, and crystal brooks,
With silken lines, and silver hooks.

John Donne

*Age does not protect you from love.
But love, to some extent,
protects you from age.*

Jeanne Moreau

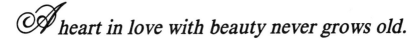 *heart in love with beauty never grows old.*

Turkish Proverb

*The heart of the old is
always young in two things,
in love for the world and length of hope.*

Mohammed

$\mathscr{M}$y most brilliant achievement
was my ability to be able to
persuade my wife to marry me.

Winston Churchill

*The secrets of success are
a good wife and a steady job.
My wife told me.*

Howard Nemerov

The best way to hold a man is in your arms.

Mae West

$\mathscr{K}$eep your eyes wide open before marriage,
and half-shut afterwards.

Benjamin Franklin

Love requires respect and friendship as well as passion. Because there comes a time when you have to get out of bed.

Erica Jong

To marry a woman or man for beauty is like buying a house for its coat of paint.

American Proverb

Friendship is love with understanding.

Origin Unknown

In the limitless desert of love, sensual pleasure has an ardent but very small place, so incandescent that at first one sees nothing else.

Colette

*The one charm of marriage is that
it makes a life of deception
absolutely necessary for both parties.*

Oscar Wilde

We are born for love.
It is the principle of existence and its only end.

Benjamin Disraeli

*If love is the answer,
could you please rephrase the question?*

Lily Tomlin

*Whoever said marriage is
a fifty-fifty proposition
doesn't know the half of it.*

*Love preserves beauty,
and the flesh of woman is fed with caresses
as are bees with flowers.*

Anatole France

The most precious possession
that ever comes to a man in
this world is a woman's heart.

*Love is the master key that opens
the gates of happiness.*

Oliver Wendell Holmes

A wise lover values not so much the gift of the lover as the love of the giver.

Thomas a Kempis

It is not a lack of love, but a lack of friendship that makes unhappy marriages.

Nietzsche

Love comforteth like sunshine after rain.

Shakespeare

I have lived long enough to know
that the evening glow of love has
its own riches and splendor.

Benjamin Disraeli

*Marriage is that relation between
man and woman in which
independence is equal,
the dependence is mutual,
and the obligation is reciprocal.*

Louis Kaufman Anspacher

*Music I heard with you
was more than music
And bread I broke with you
was more than bread.*

Love is a fire, but whether it is going to warm your hearth or burn down your house, you can never tell.

Joan Crawford

*K*isses kept are wasted;
Love is to be tasted.

Edmund Vance

Never a lip is curved with pain
That can't be kissed into smiles again.

Bret Harte

The sound of a kiss is not
so loud as that of a cannon,
but its echo lasts a great deal longer.

Oliver Wendell Holmes

Romance cannot be put into quantity production — the moment love becomes casual, it becomes commonplace.

Frederick Lewis Allen

If you would be loved,
love and be lovable.

Benjamin Franklin

A caress is better than a career.

Elisabeth Marbury

No love so true as love that dies untold.

Oliver Wendell Holmes

The reason that husbands and wives
do not understand each other is because
they belong to different sexes.

Dorothy Dix

The riches of the heart cannot be stolen.

Russian Proverb

*Passion, though a bad regulator,
is a powerful spring.*

Emerson

*Bee to the blossom, moth to the flame;
Each to his passion; what's in a name?*

Helen Hunt Jackson

In love, one first deceives
oneself and then others —
and that is what is called romance.

John L. Balderston

*Romance, like a ghost, eludes touching.
It is always where you were,
not where you are.*

George William Curtis

He loved the twilight that surrounds
The borderland of old romance.

Henry Wadsworth Longfellow

*Marriage should be a duet —
when one sings, the other claps.*

Joe Murray

More marriages might survive if
the partners realized that sometimes the
better comes after the worse.

Doug Larson

Marrying a man is like buying something you've been admiring for a long time in a shop window. You may love it when you get it home, but it doesn't always go with everything else in the house.

Jean Kerr

*If you cannot inspire a woman
with love of you,
fill her above the rim with love of herself —
all that runs over will be yours.*

Charles Caleb Colton

*𝓛et men tremble to win the hand of woman,
unless thy win along with it the
utmost passion of her heart!*

Nathanial Hawthorne

The heart has such an influence over the understanding that it is worth while to engage it in our interest.

Lord Chesterfield

If love be timid it is not true.

Spanish Proverb

Love is above all, the gift of oneself.

Jean Anouilh

*Among those whom I like or admire,
I can find no common denominator,
but among those whom I love, I can:
all of them make me laugh.*

W. H. Auden

Many waters cannot quench love,
neither can floods drown it.

Song of Solomon 8:7

When *you love someone all your saved-up*
wishes start coming out.

Elizabeth Bowen

Whoso loves
Believes the impossible.

Elizabeth Barrett Browning

*T*is sweet to know there is an eye will mark
Our coming, and look brighter when we come.

Byron

*F*riendship often ends in love;
but love in friendship — never.

Charles Caleb Colton

*Love is the irresistible desire
to be desired irresistibly.*

Louis Ginsberg

*We must resemble each other a little
in order to understand each other,
but we must be a little different
to love each other.*

Paul Geraldy

*Immature love says:
"I love you because I need you."
Mature love says:
"I need you because I love you."*

Try to reason about love and you will lose your reason.

French Proverb

Love makes the time pass.
Time makes love pass.

French Proverb

Pleasure of love lasts but a moment,
Pain of love lasts a lifetime.

If there's delight in love, 'tis when I see
That heart which others bleed for,
bleed for me.

William Congreve

Never love with all your heart,
It only ends in aching.

Countee Cullen

Special Agent Gumby falls into the frustrated hands
of the enemy.

use quote
for Linda in
Death of a
Salesman.

*With love one can live
even without happiness.*

Dostoevsky

The anger of lovers renews their love.

Terence

Nothing spoils romance so much as a sense of humor in the woman.

Oscar Wilde

A relationship is what happens between two people who are waiting for something better to come along.

*K*issing is a means of getting two people so
close together that they can't see anything
wrong with each other.

Rene Yasenik

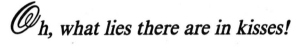

Oh, what lies there are in kisses!

Heinrich Heine

In love there are two evils: war and peace.

Horace (65-8 B.C.)

Love is what happens to men and women
who don't know each other.

W. Somerset Maugham (1874-1963)

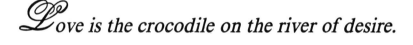

Love is the crocodile on the river of desire.

Bhartrihari (ca. 625)

There is no they, only us.

I wasn't kissing her,
I was whispering in her mouth.

Chico Marx

In a great romance, each person basically plays a part that the other really likes.

Elizabeth Ashley

*L*ove, or fear, is a great thing.

Irish Proverb

A lover without indiscretion
is no lover at all.

Thomas Hardy (1840-1928)

Love is the only game not called on account of darkness.

M. Hirschfield

*Love is an obsessive delusion
that is cured by marriage.*

Dr. Karl Bowman (1888-1973)

Love is being stupid together.

Paul Valery (1871-1945)

$\mathscr{L}$ove is the delusion that one woman differs from another.

H. L. Mencken (1880-1956)

$\mathscr{L}$ove is what you've been through with somebody.

James Thurber *(1894-1961)*

The best cure for hypochondria is to forget about your body and get interested in somebody else's.

Goodman Ace (1899-1982)

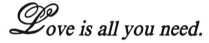

Love is all you need.

Lennon and McCartney

$\mathcal{L}$ove is like the magic touch of stars.

Walter Benton

*Love is a passport to the impossible,
so do not be disturbed if the
seas are sometimes rough.*

Lois Wyse

To love is nothing . . .
To be loved is something . . .
To love, and be loved is everything.

Love puts the fun in together . . .
the sad in apart . . .
the hope in tomorrow . . .
the joy in a heart.

*Whoever has a heart full of love
always has something to give.*

Pope John XXIII

*Real love begins where
nothing is expected in return.*

Antoine de Saint - Exupery

The best gifts are tied with heart strings.

*Once we have learned to love,
we will have learned to live.*

The entire sum of existence is the magic of being needed by just one person.

*L*ove . . .
if you have it,
you don't need anything else . . .
and if you don't have it,
it doesn't much matter what else you have.

Sir James M. Barrie

Now abideth faith, hope, love, these three;
but the greatest of these is love.

I Corinthians 13:13

Love cannot be forced . . .
Love cannot be coaxed and teased.
It comes out of Heaven
unmasked and unsought.

Pearl Buck

$\mathscr{L}$ove is a second life;
it grows into the soul, warms every vein,
and beats in every pulse.

Joseph Addison

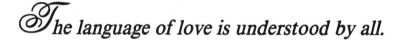

The language of love is understood by all.

That which is loved is always beautiful.

Norwegian Proverb

*A life without love is
like a year without summer.*

Swedish Proverb

$\mathcal{B}$etter an empty purse than an empty heart.

German Proverb

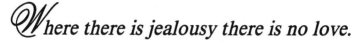

Where there is jealousy there is no love.

German Proverb

*The deep sea can be fathomed,
but who knows the hearts of men?*

Malay Proverb

A broken hand works but
not a broken heart.

Persian Proverb

He who has two loves must lie to one.

Portugese Proverb

The more violent the love,
the more violent the anger.

Burmese Proverb

My love is like a red red rose
That's newly sprung in June;
Oh, my love is like the melodie
That's sweetly played in tune.

Robert Burns

Love knows hidden paths.

German Proverb

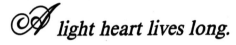 *A light heart lives long.*

Irish Proverb